THE HOPI

A TRUE BOOK

by
Andrew Santella

Children's Press®
A Division of Scholastic Inc.

New York Toronto London Auckland Sydney
Mexico City New Delhi Hong Kong
Danbury, Connecticut

A Hopi child in native dress

Reading Consultant
Nanci R. Vargus, Ed.D.
Primary Multiage Teacher
Decatur Township Schools
Indianapolis, IN

Content Consultant
Dr. Ruth J. Krochock
Archaeologist
Davis, California

The photograph on the cover shows a Hopi woman watering her crops. The photograph on the title page shows a Hopi woman carrying water.

Library of Congress Cataloging-in-Publication Data

Santella, Andrew.
   The Hopi / by Andrew Santella
      p.   cm. – (A True book)
   Includes bibliographical references and index.
   Summary: Describes the Hopi way of life, including their villages, families, farms, and reaction to white settlers.
   ISBN 0-516-22501-4 (lib. bdg.)   0-516-26987-9 (pbk.)
   1. Hopi Indians—History—Juvenile literature. 2. Hopi Indians—Social life and customs—Juvenile literature. [1. Hopi Indians. 2. Indians of North America—Arizona.] I. Title. II. Series.

E99.H7 S85 2002
979.1004'9745—dc21   2001032299

5 6 7 8 9 10 R 11 10 09 08   62

Contents

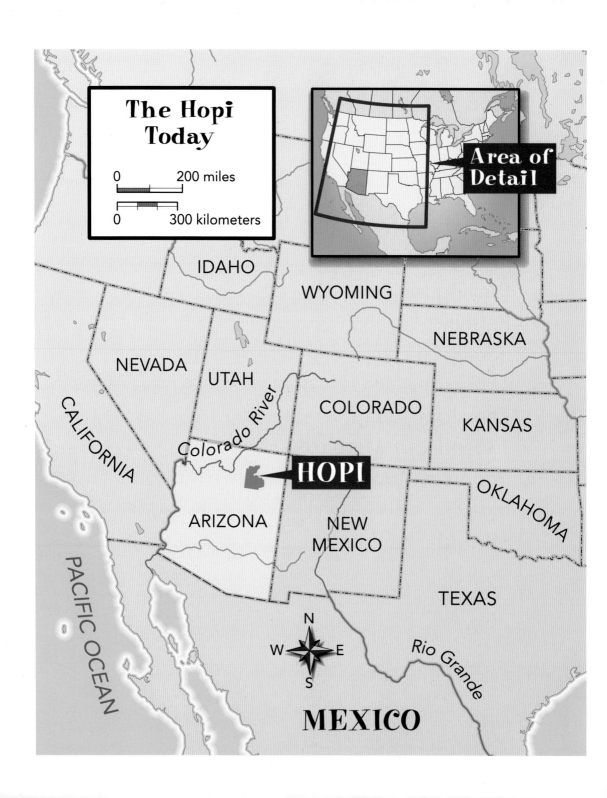

The Hopi
Today

0 ——————— 200 miles

0 ——————— 300 kilometers

Area of
Detail

IDAHO

WYOMING

NEBRASKA

NEVADA

UTAH

COLORADO

KANSAS

CALIFORNIA

Colorado River

HOPI

OKLAHOMA

ARIZONA

NEW
MEXICO

TEXAS

PACIFIC OCEAN

N
W   E
S

Rio Grande

MEXICO

Living in the Desert

The Hopi live in northeastern Arizona. They have lived in the desert there for at least one thousand years. Very little rain falls in the desert. Raising crops and keeping animals is very difficult because there is so little water. Still, the Hopi have survived and stayed in their homeland. The Hopi settled in a village called Old Oraibi (o RAY bi) around the year 1100. They have lived there ever since. This makes it one of the oldest villages in North America.

Today the Hopi live mainly in villages on top of **mesas** (MAY sas). A mesa is a tall cliff with steep sides and a flat top. Mesas are common in the deserts of the southwestern United States. The Hopi live in clay and stone houses that can be three or more stories high.

Many Hopi villages are located on top of tall mesas (top). The Hopi live in clay and stone houses that may be several stories high (bottom).

The houses stand side by side and form streets. Those streets surround a central **plaza**. A plaza is an open area used for public dances and ceremonies.

Each village is governed by a kikmongwi (kik MON wee) or village chief. He oversees **rituals** and ceremonies. Village chiefs are selected by village councils, which are made up of leaders of each clan. A clan is a large group of related

Hopi villages can be fairly large.

people. The village chief serves
for life, but can be removed
from office by the council.

The Hopi are part of a larger group of American Indians called the Pueblo.

The Hopi are part of a larger group of American Indians called the Pueblo. Pueblo is the Spanish word for village. Some villages in the southwestern United States are called pueblos. All the Pueblo people share certain traditions and ways of life. The Hopi are different from other Pueblo people in one important way. The Hopi are the only Pueblo people to speak Hopi—a language that is not related to any other Pueblo language.

Praying for Rain

The Hopi take their name from a word that means "peaceful people." According to a very old Hopi belief, the Hopi climbed up to the surface of Earth through three underground worlds. The Hopi remember that story today in their religious practices. Many

The entrance to a kiva has a ladder that leads below the ground.

of their ceremonies are performed in underground rooms
called kivas (KEY vas).

Each Hopi village contains two to six kivas. Kivas are built to remind the Hopi of their climb to the surface of Earth. A ladder made from a pine tree leads down into the entrance of the kiva. On the floor of each kiva is a small hole. This hole is called the *sipapu*. It reminds the Hopi of the hole that humans crawled through to reach the surface of Earth. Religious ceremonies are performed on the floor of the

The inside of a kiva

kiva. Just above the floor is a raised platform for people watching the ceremonies.

15

The Hopi pray for rain in the dry desert so that people, plants, and animals can live there. The Hopi believe that they must help bring rain by praying to kachinas (ka CHEE nas). Kachinas are the spirits of the **ancestors** of the Hopi. The Hopi believe that kachinas hear their prayers for rain and carry them to the gods.

Sometimes Hopi men dress as kachinas for religious ceremonies. The Hopi also make kachina dolls. The Hopi believe that if they show respect to the kachinas, their

Kachina dolls

ancestors will provide them with the rain they need to live. Kachina dolls are often decorated with pictures of clouds or lightning bolts or other things that have to do with rainfall.

Kachina Dolls

According to tradition, Hopi men carve kachina dolls from the roots of cottonwood trees. The dolls represent spirits of ancestors who hear Hopi prayers and pass them along to the gods. The dolls are usually given to women and girls during the dances. The dolls are not toys, however. They are made to teach children about Hopi spirits.

Kachina dolls are given to children to teach them about Hopi spirits.

Farming

Even though they live in the dry desert, the Hopi have always been successful farmers. They have learned to make use of every source of water. They plant their fields in valley bottoms where the rain from heavy thunderstorms collects. They dig small, deep holes and plant many

The Hopi are able to grow many crops in the desert. Seeds are planted together so that plants can survive the desert winds.

seeds in each hole. Because the seeds are planted together, the plants grow in clumps and can survive strong desert winds.

Because the seeds are planted deep in the ground, they are able to soak up water trapped deep in the soil.

In the desert, wind sometimes blows sand into piles that collect against the walls of the mesas. These piles of sand are called dunes. The Hopi have learned to plant crops here. Water can collect deep inside the dunes, so the Hopi plant crops with long roots there. If the plants' roots grow deep

Hopi even plant crops in the sand. Some plants can tolerate the dry environment.

into the dunes, they can take in that moisture.

To keep wind from damaging plants, the Hopi learned to build walls of brush around their crops.

The Hopi grow beans, squash, and melons. But the most important crop of all to the Hopi has always been corn. The Hopi grow as many as twenty-four varieties of corn. Hopi corn looks different from corn found in a supermarket. It is especially suited to grow in the desert. Its roots can grow as long as 20 feet (6 meters) to help it reach water underground. Its leaves are tough to protect the plant from strong winds.

Corn is the Hopis' most important crop.

Family Life

When a Hopi man marries, he goes to live with the family of his wife's mother. When a man and woman have children, the children become members of their mother's clan. Hopi clans are named for animals, birds, or objects. Some Hopi clan names are Sparrow, Sand,

A clan is the Hopi name for a large, extended family.

Cactus, and Bear. Individual people do not own land, but their clans do. According to

Clans often mark their land with stones bearing their symbol.

tradition, each clan's land is marked by stones bearing the symbol of the clan.

At traditional Hopi marriages, both the bride and groom must give special gifts.

The bride and her relatives prepare huge baskets full of corn cakes. They also make tubs full of corn pudding. Corn represents fruitfulness and life to the Hopi. At the

A bride's family passes gifts to a groom's family before the wedding.

same time, the groom and his male relatives make clothes out of cotton for the bride to wear at the wedding ceremony.

After they are married, husbands and wives have their own duties. Men traditionally farm and hunt for rabbits and other small animals. They also take care of the tools and equipment needed for farming and hunting. Women prepare food, make pottery, and take care of the family's children.

Farming is typically considered a man's job in Hopi society (top). Women are in charge of crafts, such as pottery and basket weaving (left).

Children become part of Hopi society as soon as they are born. A baby spends the

A baby is named by its grandmother in a special ceremony.

first nineteen days of his or her life indoors, away from visitors. The baby is given a name in a ceremony held on the twentieth day of its life. In the naming ceremony, the mother's mother bathes the child and wraps it in a blanket. Each of the baby's aunts then rubs a mix of corn-meal and water into the baby's hair. They each suggest a name and the grandmother picks one. Then, at sunrise, the family intro-duces the baby to the sun god.

Children are a special part of the Hopi society.

Hopi Pottery

The Hopi have made pottery for hundreds of years. They take clay from the desert and mold it into whatever shape they want. Then they heat the clay over a fire to make it into hard pottery. Today, the work of Hopi artists is highly valued all over the world.

The Arrival of Outsiders

The Hopi lived as they pleased in their desert home until Spanish explorers arrived in the 1540s. The Spanish built **missions** near the Hopi and tried to make them practice Christianity. The Hopi joined other Pueblo people in a revolt against the Spanish in 1680.

The Hopi were forced to leave their homes and build new ones.

They drove the Spanish away for a brief time. But just twelve years later, the Spanish regained control of the area. In order to be left alone, the Hopi moved to the tops of tall mesas. They built their villages there, with only one path leading up, so they would be easy to defend.

But the Hopi could not avoid contact with strangers. In the 1800s, settlers and soldiers from the United States made their way into the area. By 1882, the United States formed a **reservation** for the Hopi. The Hopi reservation is in

The Hopi reservation was formed in 1882.

northeastern Arizona. Their land is completely surrounded by the Navajo reservation. Over the years, the Hopi and the Navajo have argued about ownership of land.

A Hopi Olympian

Louis Tewanima was a Hopi track athlete who set the world's record in the 10,000-meter race at the 1912 Olympics. He held the record for more than fifty years. After the Olympics, Tewanima returned to the reservation to tend sheep.

Long after he set world track records, Louis Tewanima (left) poses with Robert Mathias, another Olympic athlete.

The Hopi Today

Despite the lack of rain in the desert, many Hopi remain dedicated farmers. Corn is still a very important crop. They also grow wheat, beans, onions, melons, squash, peaches, and apricots. Other Hopi raise sheep and cattle. Still others work as coal miners.

Raising sheep on the Hopi reservation (above). Hopi and Navajo children learn about computers in class (left).

For the children there are six elementary schools, a junior high school, and a high school. Some attend a nearby community college.

The Hopi live in thirteen villages located on top of three mesas. Once Hopi villages were connected only by trails. Now planes, cars, and computers connect the Hopi to the wider world. There is even an airport on the Hopi reservation. The Hopi built a cultural center on the reservation in 1970. There is also a shopping mall, a hotel, and restaurants. Many tourists travel to the

Children listen to a presentation in a Hopi museum.

ancient Hopi village of Oraibi to learn about Hopi traditions.

To Find Out More

Here are some additional resources to help you learn more about the Hopi:

 **Books**

Bonvillain, Nancy. **The Hopi.** Chelsea House, 1995.

Kamma, Anne. **If You Lived With the Hopi.** Scholastic, 1999.

Sneve, Virginia Driving Hawk. **The Hopis.** Holiday House, 1995.

Spears, Bryan. **The Hopi Indians.** Chelsea House, 1994.

Organizations and Online Sites

Hopi Cultural Center
P.O. Box 67
Second Mesa, Arizona
86043
520-734-2401

**Hopi Cultural
Preservation Office**
www.nau.edu/~hcpo-p

Links to articles about Hopi
arts, farming, and other
topics.

**The Hopi of the
Southwest**
*www.clpgh.org/cmnh/
exhibits/north-south-east-
west/hopi*

An online exhibit of the
Carnegie Museum of
Natural History.

**Rainmakers from
the Gods**
*www.peabody.harvard.edu/
katsina/default.html*

Information on Hopi
kachinas.

Important Words

ancestors people who came before

kachina special dancer who imitates the spirits

kiva underground chamber where special ceremonies take place

mesa a raised area of land that has steep slopes and a flat top

mission a religious group that travels to new areas to spread their faith

plaza a public square in a city or town

reservation an area of land that has been set aside for a group of people to live on

ritual a special way to do something, often part of a ceremony

Index

Meet the Author

Andrew Santella writes for *Gentlemen's Quarterly, the New York Times Book Review*, and other publications. He is also the author of several Children's Press titles.